Southern
Messenger
Poets

Dave Smith, Editor

CELESTIAL BODIES

ℂ POEMS

Sidney Wade

Louisiana State University Press ⚜ *Baton Rouge*

2002

for Selcuk Altun
with gratitude and affection

Copyright © 1997, 1998, 1999, 2000, 2001, 2002 by Sidney Wade

All rights reserved

Manufactured in the United States of America

First printing

11   10   09   08   07   06   05   04   03   02

5   4   3   2   1

Designer: Melanie O'Quinn Samaha

Typeface: ACaslon

Printer and binder: Thomson-Shore, Inc.

ISBN 0-8071-2824-4 (cloth); ISBN 0-8071-2825-2 (paperback)

The author offers grateful acknowledgment to the editors of the following publica-
tions, in which some of the poems herein first appeared, sometimes in slightly differ-
ent form: *Atlanta Review, Bomb, Chattahoochee Review, Denver Quarterly, Disquieting
Muses* (e-zine), *Drunken Boat* (e-zine), *Gettysburg Review, Gulf Coast, Kitaplik*
(Turkey), *Metropolitan Review, New England Review, New Republic, Paris Review,
Southern Review, Thumbscrew* (England).

The paper in this book meets the guidelines for permanence and durability of the
Committee on Production Guidelines for Book Longevity of the Council on Library
Resources. ⊗

CONTENTS

☾

CELESTIAL BODIES

Heart and Soul

Heart   Such beauty in the world, O mutinous giver—
              snow on the rose, the golden river . . .

Soul   You loiter now, old fox, old friend,
              but you know what happens in the end.

Heart   I know the honey in the spheres.
              I know the blessing in the cup.
              I know the conjugated years.
              I know the jig is up.

Soul   Come empty in this black repose,
              the center of the turning world.
              Leave vex, leave yatter, come and sit,
              our wordless conscience furled.

Heart   My fingers shade the blazing sand.
              My deserts blow with apple trees.
              A heart can change in time and does,
              a heart will take its changing ease.

Soul   You understand my constancy,
              inhuman in its scope, which marks
              and coddles everything, which parks
              the brilliant warp of vision in the dark.

Heart   I know. But world to body sings.
              That ragged song is ravishing.

Wind in the Roses

that old romantic cosmos
is the origin of our excellent despair

wind spanks through it
keening the edge of desire

branches jerk away from the shine
leaves of grass turn their backs

shimmy and slur, shimmy and slur
a constant and variable affair

it whips things away
so kings have no tents

and I have no clothes
I wish we were infinitely pure

but at this speed the shimmer is intense
things get better and already they're lost

like irresponsible kissing
this bright disaster spilling forward

Mouth-River

I want to raise some notes from the under-mind
and fan the rumors at bed-time
the beautiful word-fall that churns up from a ripe center

I want I want I want
rises from the fire diaphragm
laps on the shores of the throat and rides out on the tongue

tête et amour
immensity and pleasure-dew
are better than a bank full of pretty money

there's enough beauty in this world to choke a god

A Million Galaxies and a Little Song

My poem children are running wild
they scatter from me like cockeyed hares

this one is charging the upright vacuum cleaner
that one has taken one hundred and forty dollars

and five more are eating dried figs in a ring
so I'm just sitting here with my green olives

and singing *all greeny grow the rushes-O*
but I'd like to sing about that heavy gold river

about the crow on the bank and his golden eye
I'd like to sing about these great whanging sheets of light

but all of a sudden it's too bright to see
and here's another one dashing off into the glare

Rain Heart

I've been dry many days
rain heart

why don't you come whispering up
and loosen that structural tie

I'll go stand by the ocher-colored river
and watch for your still blue mouth

I think it's time to put lightning in its place
in the blueprint of your veins

I think it's time to cry through the windows
and through the house-high weeds

I think it's time to translate the pleasure of being found
into a damp stellar language

I think it's time to dissolve so I guess I'll pour my all into the vessels
                                   of Paradise Manor
plink plink plink

Engagement

Once I had a common flirtation with Life.
I had a softer skill in turning from the edge, then.

In the world where you live, I learned a body-version of love.
I took pleasure in that natural talking.

Your figure was draped in fulfillment robes.
Hot and difficult to touch.

We found some mutual degradation in our high pure dance,
a practical mixture of fear and loathing.

Then I learned that I'm bound but not forever.
That I can pass in utter concourse through a windowless vision.

This gave me a minute of basic buoyance.
My voices told me *the egg's in the oven,*

enjoy the soul-slump, toy with the drain.
Sit on that withered stump under the pleasure-dome.

Even though it's the radiance that counts,
Immolation-In-The-Heart-Fire is a grim machine.

Divina Rule

We're bound
old tramp mate
partner in the house museum
through post-product depression
through Swindle City
we've lived in tatters and grace
in the archival hive
but now it's all clanging
it's a change of health
it's a pleat song on a rip tide
a remarkable passage
the owls have arrived
and they're staring hard
it means something august
so let's drive out the bee-words
and hang on to our sweet
and gangly luggage

Chin Song

Let me confess:
      in this prefabricated world,
            in among the 10 million replacement parts,

I am a creature of the comforts of sin.
      I like sitting on the golden fence
            that cleanly bisects the Problem Swamp.

I like a bracing game of metaphor roulette.
      On the odd, fluid, and unlit occasion,
            I indulge in an act of passionate reading.

In this province where happenstance is a major occurrence,
      I frequent the do-wop bar.
            I go dancing with my beloved at The Listening Jam

and get hot feet.
      Then we sit high on the banks of the Late Fall River
            and feel coolly debauched.

All my virtues are down there,
      swimming among others' evil grunting ways.
            But I have great intestinal fortitude

and rarely require the Paregoric of Life.
      So don't worry about me.
            Soon I'll be exploding into soul-flight

through this world-held,
      or is it word-held,
            landscape poem.

See that low purple cloud,
      that smear on the horizon?
            That's where I'll make my delicate fortune.

Un Messaggio per il Corpo

I'm busting out of this seraglio.
There are hot strawberries out west,
and I want a childish million.
I'll go pound the ponderosa
with a nobotnik or an errant male
to help undefine the moment.
This is known as the buddy-ro system.
We'll be in a large constructivist pique,
which is really a ponderosity,
but we'll make stunning progress.
We'll locate the Lakota Dharma
and slip into a vast energy warehouse.
We'll watch the eerie transfigurations
in the winter sunrise, and then we'll waltz.
Then we will disinherit the earth.
It will have been a stewy tempus.
An absolutely magnificent failure.
What a wonderful waste.
I love this phase.

Little Body Songs

A very cool guy
in a paper smoulder he
speaks the true language of nerve

                              Ah teach me to sing
                              tick song and reggae
                              sit down and toy with my mouth

I'm ravenous and
he puts on digestive airs
it's one big exhaust bar, man

                              Girls in bras in cars
                              and golden guys go crazy

There's a blue-green globe
in the pupil of my eye
it's called a hurricane patch

                              Now here is a voice
                              a joy mover it's coming
                              for me the deep guest

Esther Merveille and
her marvellous bee
a bee abeille oh boy

                              Oh mercy he is
                              singing good let's feel his ear

Lotos hand swollen
red plum it's a body joy
not to be toppled by thought.

Blank Studious Form on the Virgin Highway

a young man stands looking at the sky

he works all day at the nightmare factory so he's got a steady nightmare
  income

one day he decides to go stand in the presence of Desire

a snowstorm of pleasure interferes with his brain

he displays his ritual passions

nothing happens

upon his return he's asked *did you find everything missing?*

he says *yes*

he heads over to the transcendental meditation station

this is a good stalling area he thinks

Desire wanders by and stands listening outside the small golden trembling
  windows

O baby-o he says to the emptiness that shadows Desire

murmur me a heart secret and then step aside

you're blocking the stellar lune

At the Movies, Once,

I stood in a hot line.
Ahead of me were the Harpies.
From in there we could smell the desert.

They were thinking of abandoning the flesh-tongue.
I asked them if I should write with a kind of liquid joy, or maybe a wolf.

Engage the right hand for sonic purposes, they said.
Write us a song.
Make like Edith Piaf sitting in a rusty tin.

Pardon my math, grand-mère, I interjected,
but I'm just a wee body wandering the open range of sound.

When desire raises its pointy little head,
you've got to finger it, they said, and shrugged.
But then, instead of disastering, you could just hope.

Nope, I said.
You bring the bucket and I'll bring the mop.
Let's sing us some torch songs and swab this abnormally blue moon.

Ideology Stinks, but the Heart Smells Pure

I'd been living for years with an adolescent boy,
investing in yachts and party suits, that sort of thing,
when a real convergence struck me:
where there is scarcity in the boudoir

and malevolence in the pit of the stomach,
it's time to do the disappearing unit.
I did.
I belted in my eyeballs,

did some marginal hoofing,
and leaped off a nearby precipice.
I sailed by the relics of an overblown landscape
until I stumbled onto Happenstance College.

This is what I saw:
an abstract god lounging on the lawn on a starry blanket.
Sometimes he got up to paint on no apparent easel.
He pondered the question of the Happiness Game

and decided it couldn't be renewed.
This was an anorectic rex, I decided,
not much interested in radicalization of the spirit.
So I moved on.

Clutching my small, heartfelt purse,
I headed for the mirrored academy
to study the politics of exile and engagement.
Here, in the absence of desire,

I realized at once that the dervish of my heart
ached with more thought than usual,
and so I moved on once more.
A fever of angels assailed me and spoke:

show your bare feet and we'll negotiate.
So I did and they did,
and after some enormous lunch dates on Sundays
I began to smell optimism in the nearsomeness

of genuine mouth-to-mouth intelligence.
I understood now how the hand of desire
will always reach for the purple heart-candy
and that, most of all, this is a miracle of design.

And that perfection is most basically mild.
So now we can examine my many disenthornments
and have some romantic fruitcake.
Come on over here and join me, you mild slickered bird.

Plainsong

here is something
from the government catastrophe loop
it's perdurable
it's reprehensible in plastic
it's made of weapons-grade linoleum
it's a rapid-fire song
whose principal parts
are pounding the floodplain
as we speak
it's three or four hundred pages long
and it takes many days to decompose
what it really is is
secret secret secret secret

Approaching Fifty

I'm not doing any of that *croning* shit, I can
tell you right now.
> —Donna M.

I've graduated from behavioral college.
I've met my share of cataclysmic goof-balls.
I've been wheeled in to the emergency era
and introduced to the triumph report.
Insurance enablers line the highway to disaster,
where I'm leaning now on a motionless stick.
I'm looking for the great high words,
but what comes are *mumbledy peg* and *washing machine*.
I smell a crude ruined smell.
It's a slice of wince pie.
I am handed some academic pliers
by a man with a too-proud expression on his face.
It's a kind of lesion.
He asks me to manufacture, out of all this,
an argument for stellar equality.
OK. Give me the materials and don't make me pant.
It isn't so simple. It's an amazement.

Our Hearts Transcend Us

The first time he says
I love you my tongue
clicks on my teeth
in involuntary dismay
or is it pleasure
and I wonder what to do
and what *is* love anyway
and he says *we know what love is don't we*
and I say *yes* but of course I'm bluffing
so let's see here are some possibilities
      it's a wild attitudinal policy
      it's a pretty silly lip-trick
      it's feeling light & suffering & controlled
      it's a body song
      a pleasure-tower
      a mountain of joy
      a crucible
      a westering thing
      it's a powerful antidote to fear
but then there are the awkward flying
and all those gauzy questions
it can also be a genuine miscalculation
or maybe group suffocation
it's when you leave your trendier self
and your clothes in the fast lane
and maybe end up falling and very very cold
and in the middle of all this I think
in the absence of zero there is amplitude
and then turn away to start a bonfire
which is a lot more fun with lighter fluid

Words

Just now when I asked, *How are you today, bright joy?*
it responded, *I'm tard. I'm sticky and tard.*

But I don't care, because I am just about
to pour myself out into this shining river.

The wild cranes are singing their leaving song,
and I write for joy and for the heavy clouds.

I write as well for the stinging rain,
for each drop that sings a small fast song.

I write for joy and the songs and their words,
whose brilliant rainy edges fit exactly

into other brilliant rainy edges.
I just have to find the perfect match.

And when I do, they are terribly grateful.
They say they will return the great favor.

They say they will lead me straight to God.
They say, in the language of rain,

Here is God, the skeleton on which we hang our skin.
They say, *Here is God, the great open-throated river.*

Luna Moth

here is the beautiful place
transmuted by weather
rubbed down to stubble and stump

I am here
I can feel my body confidently absorbing air
dancing with the wherewithal

one can drink in words
and then drown
in their fierce pleasures

sometimes comes
a brief light hope
or the powder of love

last night a luna moth
came out of the dark to bash itself on my window
then the whatever-it-was pulled it back into the night

to entertain another
who might take it for a metaphor sandwich
and open up the port

these are the broad stakes
it will get us all
don't be afraid

THIRTEEN MOONS

I

Whole white face
In front of the black else.
The whole white world is drenched.

II

Woman moon.
Row deeper into the moon water.

III

Where is that immortal thing?
In the trees, now, naked to the waist.

IV

The Queen of the Night. White-armed and cow-eyed.
O moon O moon O moon O you are darkly shadowed meat.

V

Joyflight and joystick
Have nothing to do
With this white beauty,

VI

This beautiful female nude,
Severe and frosted to the sky.

VII

Light ices
The frozen lake
And the stiff dark woods.
Whiteness on the white snow.
A rigid cleaning.

VIII

Rise over,
Madonna of the moon,
Occasional losses.

IX

Once long ago a piece of her stone heart fell to the earth.
Her dog followed blindly.
He sits still under the snowy pines.

X

How to feed it what to feed it?
Spent food. Light food.

XI

O Pearl
Of Great Price
In the wide black hold.

XII

The moon is the mother of death and beauty.

XIII

Under the large light and its dark eaves:
Women whispering to women.

Tickets to the Grand Bizarre

are peddled for flesh-honey
in the golden system of trade.
Let's go join in the elements
and turn dross into jade
in the home of the moment
in the heart of time.
Who seeks here shall be lost,
who finds will remain
in the grand unified theory
of the body in love.
This minute is the ticket,
this minute the coin of the coil.
The world is a sensible object.
The heart beats in its soil.

Dancing at the Bin Bir Gece
Istanbul

We've bluefished, wined, succinctly smoked and drunk
of course too much and now my queer friend J
and I stroll arm in woolen arm the nightfell
street. In words as fine as feathers I
contend our other queer friend P who strolls
in rings of light before us is an angel.
J waves and snorts and says but he's my dear
a dedicated homo-seck-syu-all,
and thus we sail the fairly stable streets
to the delinquent doors of Bin Bir, a low
delighted bar, which hugely swells
with many beauteous creatures, some not so,
all ample in their finery, but first
I think I'll pee. I amble into the ladies'
and pull up stumped to see a handsome man
darken his eyes in the mirror as I've forgotten
where I am, if I ever really knew.
I turn to go but Sloe-eyes reels me back.
Oh come on in we're all girls here, and yes,
of course, I think and then I enter, flush,
depart the stall and find that in that shuttered
moment more have bloomed upon the sink.
We chatter and prink and rattle on—mascara,
blush, and men, and when they ask and I
say poet then this pressing issue hungers
up with striking eyes—do I write of *passion?*
and yes I say of course and we all soar
at this intelligence and float out on a sea
of joy, I to my angel and our earthly companion,
they to their feathery poetic evening quest
and from this black box in the night I believe I can see
how common and beautiful is the secret best
we all compose to take the next light step.

Beyazit

Dust through the plane trees and great sheets of particulate
light settling on gray slabs and paving stones—
dust on my shoes—through two thin layers of leather

the soles of my feet graze the uneven landscape
of the cobbled yard as if they were fingers and I were blind—
stepping the stones is like treading the scales

of a great old tortoise whose ridged carapace
is the visible rind of the splendid and ruined,
the much-silted surface of a lacquered past.

Chimaera

The beastly hot flesh
    of the beach's nude white sand
        sears the feet even

in the dark the waves
    a quiet lace ornament
        on hissing water

from here we climb up
    the mountain's flank it's hairless
        and strange and arid

pebbles chuckle down
    the trail is thin my flashlight
        flashes and ranges

like a wild white
    eidolon no moon hot darkness
        radiating down

aqueous lightnings
    prick at the backs of the eyes
        here is the odor

of seeping gases
    here is the face of the beast
        small fires in the ground

little blue tongues cold
    to the eye lap formally
        at the night's profile

I've stalked my way here
    to this mythical minute
        on the creature's lip

down a metaphorical path
    whose wobbly complex of wrong
        destructive pieces

and powerful beauties
    resembles this old
        monster grappled up

by sailors heaving
    on the ragged growling breast
        of an ancient sea

and now here I am
    scrambling over the stone face
        peering down into

the hot compound eyes
    and wondering from the outskirts
        of the fractured ground

if a tangle with
    the handsome Bellerophon
        on his magical

steed with the great and
    poetic wings isn't just
        what I really need

Kara Göl

Black Lake

We have climbed all day to this black eye
black lake we picnic by

In the cold light we admire the high scenery
the frozen pony the half-eaten greens

I am harder than I know and my heart is blacker
The water is silent and exact

The golden child we have hauled up with us
plays with a crazy chicken in the green grass

The sun throws down an occasional spear
My soul is green as ice and as severe

There is joy though in the coldness
It streams from the earth it bowls

down the mountain in bright exuberant ribbons
excessively bristling with wayward propositions

a constant and variable slosh in the ears
There is joy in the clarity that distance wears

like an evening gown in this unearthly altitude
whose every reflection is natural and cruel

whose fine air we relinquish in blue necessity
stepping carefully the hard line of descent

Out for a Walk

My soul took itself out for a walk the other day
It hasn't yet returned and I'm slightly concerned

      it used to say it always wanted to travel the world
      it used to say it couldn't help it if its heart was larger than the room
                                     in which we lived
      it used to say it's terrible how it longed to converse with other flesh

So what should I do?

      should I allow myself the rich dark honey of a jealous rage?
      should I breathe slowly and count to ten thousand several hundred
                                     times?
      should I harrow the black soil of my body for clues?

Perhaps I'll just sit quietly and swing my foot
Perhaps I'll just listen to this fatal thudding in my chest

Ars Longa

I

Why must art be
long, I ask?
Why not sizzle
up the task?
Largo, says the
rhapsodist,
*snappy hands make
counterfeits.*

II

Latefall light in
Florida—
intimate gold
camera.
Moistly dying
overtones
muscled up in
little bones.

III

Vita brevis,
this is why
heart lives in an
open eye,
swallowing in
hopeful bits
morsels of the
infinite.

Mirror

these woods are quiet as glass

the lake holds its cold breath

my soul is ink

and my heart is a small helicopter,
idling

the earth nailed through its core spins in a slow dark

and all the surfaces hum

I am waiting for your blue-black word

Ink

I am looking for a word from you.
I've combed the landscape of my body,
I've traveled its dark rivers.
I've looked under the cloud of my heart,
unraveled its complicated net of veins.
I've found plenty of blue material here—
why don't you write?

Backyard of the Words

Desire sits on the patio
and smokes a cigarette
in the rain

It has waited all day
for the word-made flesh
yet finds itself
at the end
alone

In the drizzle
it meditates
on things that are wet
as a thin blue line
rises in the damp light
of the streetlamp

Ah, my soul-flip

You know who you are

Time Is Money

Gray nickels up
in the east—

the forecast
is dire, but

it is a stately sight.
Dogs are whirping

at the moon in China
and a string quartet

has rattled out
an ardent arabesque

that brings consumers
to their knees.

Here is a common heresy:
Things are Bleak.

See here—this bag
of olives on my lap

is radiating happily
its currency.

Let's slurp it up
in unison

and celebrate
inflation for a change.

And racket.
Let's celebrate as well

that quarter
where wind smells

like wet steel
and the children

laugh unshod and holler
through their hands.

Where epistemology
is chocolate

and bags of olives
mean a lot.

Where black
moons flower

in the desert.
Where power

of attorney
counts for nothing.

Where time is racing
through the sluicegates,

every second
riotous in diamonds.

This world is burning
up in beauty.

Time Sandwich

Come grab a spoon and eat,
you tempting old thing.
I've got comfortable salad
and squirrel in the fridge
or, if you prefer,
beef swirl in delinquent sauces.
I've had it with deadlines
and other insults to humanity,
so let's go stand on the porch
with a tub full of spinach.
I'm on the cusp of enlightenment
and I'll tell you what I know:
there's an awfully fine line between
the here and the not-here.
What I really want
is to live and eat forever.
Let's biodegrade, OK?
Then we can approach
that smoky apparition
and give it a piece of our mind:
be careful in carting away the bones—
they may still be capable of grief.

Time As Interlocutor

Time in its sweater
regards me curiously,
inquires after

my inner weather.
*It's a little drizzly and
showery. There's some*

*volcanic action
and a high blood tide, but soon
the old blind boy will*

sing at the light stump,
I say, *and then the weather
will be spiky.* Ah.

Time and a Dog

All right we can't repeat the past
don't want to bones are in the grass
time and a dog regard them mildly
sniff and pass on to other piles
what's round the bend is *entre nous*
mon ancien amour, mon âme I'm through
with *dies irae* through with twirping
on about the mess the bird
has turned the dog has yapped the heart
has swollen in the cage and partly
mooned it's almost full it's time
to wash the hands and look sublime

CELESTIAL BODIES

Night Air, Bokhara,

is tantalizing as romance with a capital R
I am drunk and absurd it is fantastically sweet

to reel out alone under the soft black sheet
of this sky past the bloodbag of the Emir's Ark

sort of dancing with my besotted self and some fine old fantasies
and then pull up stupefied at the pure clarity of the line

of the mosque's silhouette on this impossible sky
whose stars drill severely through the black expanse

and I continue my roll and wish for much more
than the reasonable thing which of course if granted

would obliterate me but still there's this sirening
dream of bliss that keeps the heart in a hanker

even though the road you're assigned is an austere kind
and the overall balance a tricky sport

Ant, Kantharos, Bunch of Grapes

On the older shores of the firmament,
on the porch of complex and starry affairs,

a thoughtful insect traverses the figure
of the Mother of Seasons on her ample urn.

He samples a draft of the dark blue vintage
and remembers the line on the bare feet of angels

rushing through fields of convolvulus,
whose twining stems and pallid blooms

bind up the limbs of those whose ambitions
propel them heavenward, and hold them firm.

He shoulders a passage from the darker canticles
and sings in a language that surges with love

for black rains at night and for brilliant wine,
for green-eyed voices in the seething grass.

Narrowness is Pain, says Gurudev

we're lapping up the contemplative life
here in our peerless ashram

where half-day inlets shimmer
between life and betrayal

some of us came with our cats
others with blonde derangements

my over-soul in rubber galoshes
sneaked in a flask of uncertainty

it aches my temple
it Xes my heart

I'm proud however of my
thoroughly deviational strategy

infect me with brilliance
I pray every day

then I wash the grass and tell all
before the stars go out

it's a regular germ-fest, friend,
in a foreign rushing dialogue

wide as the flushed and steaming brow
under my cool white hand

Beatitudes

Let me take out my magic tar-baby pencil
and scribble out for you what I saw

when I settled into that dense cloud
and caught a glimpse of God's hide.

Plainsong Anthony and the Plainclothesmen
sang in the language of stones.

Mister Mistry pulled out his bewitch stick
and berserk mazurkaed through the radiant blind.

The Rhine Maidens wheened out the required
Requiem and then ran off at the mind.

The legal ramifications of this are yet unknown,
but *I* know. I've got interstitial vision.

And sometimes I take a wisdom pill.
But this was panoramic for real.

There was passion, power, plenitude.
Low-sodium acrobatics, mind-sap, maw.

Levantine parsimony. Paternalistic flaw.
My mother's perfume: Pandemonium Marmalade.

They were all torch songs,
kind and complicated by doldrums and pang.

What they mean to say is,
You are the higher goods, Ignotus.

You are a magnificent fool.
Let's entwinkle. Star Star Star.

Sundog to Moondog

You teach and sing, my friend. I think that's why you need a drink.
You got one foot in the sublime, the other prinked
in acrobatic shoes. C'mon pal, lose
the stuffy props. It's time you whapped your tail
in time to some rhapsodic blues.

OK then son, I lift my glass of palest ale.
A toast to bluest rhetoric, a toast to stumpy you.

Ah, misery, my friend, is grand, if threaded very fine.
A heart in hanker heated up is sweet and unbenign.

And unbeknownst to us.

Ah, yes.
Would wunst upon a time the gods could jimmy ope
the hole that keeps celestial types a million years, in light,
apart, and, yes, I fear, a-mope.

True Knowledge College

ah my soul-clip, where are we headed?

vast distances to the moon-store

will you open me please?
I'm greedy greedy greedy
pour in the lightening wine

I'm speaking in feathers here

I'm impatient, too

astonishment rides on small bright wings

and then?

saffron frantic soul flight

ah here it is
gleaming in at the pores
through me the membrane

Edge

my head is full of demons
they steer me to the east
and tell me to descend
I see on the broadening wall

a star a moving star
I know I must stay on the line
I find some old grottoes
and a terrifying ledge

I am dazed in the open
the light is growing scattered and dark
I hold out my heart
and begin the counting

someone asks after my soul
I remember it well
it was limpid once
hanging over my lost ground

My Istanbul

I feel mottled
a gray cloud slides

over the domes
turned from the white

sea and its secret
Greek dream

here is a white bird
and a gravedigger's spade

here is a smooth white face
here an inswept corner

here it is temporarily perfect
moon thirst and moon slake

rise out of that great lively sea
to illuminate the dim passageways

here is a star inside a bag
this is my heart beating faster

One Petrified Sunday

we all disappeared,
walked straight out of our poems
and into heaven.
We left the old breakfast things,
the pincers,
the practically perfect savings.
We found a heart stump
and an indigo eye.
It all smelled of ammonia.
The indigo eye saw a tree,
whole in front of the black else,
drenched and shining.
In a differently-bodied vision
light iced a snow-white clearing.
But the great sadness
beyond all the gadding
was this:
Paradise is wordless.
An ice palace.
And that is why
I'll reach for the apple sandwich any day,
and that old sky of ours,
blazing with stars
in the night of the 10,000 things.
I'll sing in the rusty shower stall.
I'll take my stand in the wandering room.
I'll boast at the seams.
Ah, this is hard, bright Daddy.

Pluteus Petasatus

Night. A mute white dwarf
in earthmoving hat
bulbs up from the mold.

It has nudged and shoved
its smart headstrong head
through the discrete wood.

Now its exquisite
fruiting body feeds
on the broke-down else,

infiltrates the blank
detritus of lives,
and rises and smells

like a star. This is
degenerate news,
the small moonlit kind.